Oh Glory!

11 Quilt Projects to Salute the Stars and Stripes

KATHY FLOWERS

Oh Glory! 11 Quilt Projects to Salute the Stars and Stripes
© 2017 by Kathy Flowers

Martingale®
19021 120th Ave. NE, Ste. 102
Bothell, WA 98011-9511 USA
ShopMartingale.com

Printed in China
22 21 20 19 18 17   8 7 6 5 4 3 2 1

Library of Congress Cataloging-in-Publication Data
is available upon request.

ISBN: 978-1-60468-725-5

MISSION STATEMENT

We empower makers who use fabric and yarn
to make life more enjoyable.

CREDITS

PUBLISHER AND
CHIEF VISIONARY OFFICER
Jennifer Erbe Keltner

CONTENT DIRECTOR
Karen Costello Soltys

DESIGN MANAGER
Adrienne Smitke

MANAGING EDITOR
Tina Cook

PRODUCTION MANAGER
Regina Girard

ACQUISITIONS EDITOR
Karen M. Burns

PHOTOGRAPHER
Brent Kane

TECHNICAL EDITOR
Mary Helen Schiltz

ILLUSTRATOR
Christine Erikson

COPY EDITOR
Durby Peterson

SPECIAL THANKS

Thanks to Karen and Casey Burns of Carnation, Washington, for allowing the photography for this book to take place in their home.

DEDICATION

Leo Kruger

*His kindness and sharing
with others was the thread
that bound him to family
and friends alike.*

This book is dedicated in honor and loving memory of my father, Leo Kruger. A veteran of World War II, he proudly served in the United States Navy, receiving his basic training at Naval Station Great Lakes in Illinois, before being transferred to Camp Bradford in Norfolk, Virginia. During his enlistment he served on three ships in the Pacific, the USS LST-307, the USS Eldorado (AGC-11), and the USS LST-485. He received the World War II Victory Medal, the Asiatic-Pacific Campaign Medal, and the American Campaign Medal.

He felt so strongly about serving his country during the war that he left high school before graduation during his senior year, and therefore did not receive his high school diploma. It wasn't until May 28, 2004, at the age of 78, that my father received his high school diploma from Dwight Township High School. Based on his grades many years previous, his years of military service, and the military medals he received, the high school superintendent felt it appropriate to honor my father for his service and hand him his long-forgotten diploma. To a standing ovation, this once young and vibrant man climbed the stairs aged and slow, walked across the stage, saluted, shook hands, and received his diploma, proud to be recognized as a hometown hero. The applause was thunderous. Tears filled his eyes, his hands shook as he accepted his diploma, and his lips whispered, "Thank you," as he stood facing the crowd, amazed and grateful after many long years.

My father was a proud but simple man who asked for very little throughout his life. He worked hard and long hours, most often working more than one job so my mother could always be home with us. He believed children should never come home to an empty house after school. He instilled in his children what he felt were important values. His kindness and sharing with others was the thread that bound him to family and friends alike. He passed away in 2009 after a sudden brief illness. He believed in me even when I didn't have the courage to believe in myself. I was honored to call him my dad, and I now pay respect to him by sharing with you my quilt designs so that you may honor all the men and women in your life who have proudly served our country. It is their selflessness in serving our great country that provides us with our daily freedoms. Thank you!

Contents

Introduction

Who can resist a splash of red, white, and blue to display American patriotism? And what better way to say thank you to all the military members of your family and friends than decorating your home with patriotic colors? You don't have to wait until the Fourth of July to celebrate or show your pride.

Oh Glory! is a collection of patriotic quilts and small quilted projects to enjoy. Regardless of your level of quilting expertise, you'll find something here for everyone. For example, "Pappa Bear," the largest quilt, was designed with the beginning quilter in mind, while "Stars of Freedom," one of the smaller quilts, was designed for more advanced quilters. To make a patriotic quilt, simply use fabrics from red, white, and blue color families. Red might become maroon or rust. White could be cream or beige. Blue might be navy or sky blue. Your fabrics might not even feature patriotic motifs. As long as they blend nicely, you have the colors of Americana!

Every day we are America—home of the brave, land of the free. The threads that bind all these quilts are honor and pride. Honor your military member, whether it is your husband, brother, sister, or friend. Display your completed project with pride.

God bless America!

Song of Victory

Make a throw or wall hanging that highlights two classic blocks: the Martha Washington Star and Friendship Star. A combination of simple prints in red, cream, and blue allows the striking graphic elements to take center stage. Add a bold red-and-cream piano-key border to carry through the theme of stars and stripes.

"Song of Victory," designed by Kathy Flowers

FINISHED QUILT: 43½" x 43½"

FINISHED BLOCKS:
Large Martha Washington Star: 9" x 9"
Small Martha Washington Star: 6" x 6"
Friendship Star: 6" x 6"

★ **MATERIALS**

Yardage is based on 42"-wide fabric.

1⅓ yards of red print for blocks, border, and binding
1⅛ yards of cream print for blocks and border
⅞ yard of beige print for blocks and border
⅝ yard of blue print for blocks
3 yards of fabric for backing
53" x 53" piece of batting

CUTTING

From the cream print, cut:
4 strips, 1¾" x 42"
1 strip, 3½" x 42"; crosscut into 4 squares, 3½" x 3½"; cut the squares into quarters diagonally to yield 16 A triangles
1 strip, 3⅛" x 42"; crosscut into 8 squares, 3⅛" x 3⅛"; cut the squares in half diagonally to yield 16 B triangles
1 strip, 5¾" x 42"; crosscut into 4 squares, 5¾" x 5¾"; cut the squares into quarters diagonally to yield 16 C triangles
2 strips, 2¾" x 42"; crosscut into 20 squares, 2¾" x 2¾"; cut 4 squares into quarters diagonally to yield 16 D triangles
1 strip, 4¼" x 42"; crosscut into 4 squares, 4¼" x 4¼"; cut the squares into quarters diagonally to yield 16 E triangles
1 strip, 2⅜" x 42"; crosscut into 8 squares, 2⅜" x 2⅜"; cut the squares in half diagonally to yield 16 F triangles
1 strip, 2" x 42"; crosscut into 16 squares, 2" x 2"

From the blue print, cut:
1 strip, 3½" x 42"; crosscut into 4 squares, 3½" x 3½"; cut the squares into quarters diagonally to yield 16 A triangles
1 strip, 2⅜" x 42"; crosscut into 16 squares, 2⅜" x 2⅜"; cut the squares in half diagonally to yield 32 F triangles
3 strips, 2⅞" x 42"; crosscut into 32 squares, 2⅞" x 2⅞"
1 strip, 2½" x 42"; crosscut into 16 squares, 2½" x 2½"

Continued on page 10

Continued from page 8

From the red print, cut:

2 strips, 3⅛" x 42"; crosscut into 16 squares, 3⅛" x 3⅛";
  cut the squares in half diagonally to yield 32 B triangles

1 strip, 2¾" x 42"; crosscut into 4 squares, 2¾" x 2¾";
  cut the squares into quarters diagonally to yield 16 D
  triangles

8 strips, 1⅞" x 42"

5 strips, 2½" x 42"

4 strips, 1" x 42"

From the beige print, cut:

4 strips, 2½" x 42"; crosscut into 64 squares, 2½" x 2½"

3 strips, 2⅞" x 42"; crosscut into 32 squares, 2⅞" x 2⅞"

4 strips, 1¾" x 42"

MAKING THE MARTHA WASHINGTON STAR BLOCKS

1. Align one cream A triangle atop one blue A triangle, right sides together; sew together along one short edge to make a blue-and-cream triangle unit. Press the seam allowances toward the blue triangle. Repeat to make a total of 16 blue-and-cream triangle units, always placing the blue triangle on the bottom.

2. Align one cream B triangle with one blue-and-cream triangle unit. Sew together along the long edge to make a windmill unit. Press the seam allowances toward the cream triangle. Repeat to make a total of 16 windmill units.

Make 16.

3. Lay out four windmill units as shown; join in pairs, and then press the seam allowances toward the blue triangle. Join the windmill unit pairs as shown to make a Windmill block. Press the seam allowances in one direction. Repeat to make a total of four Windmill blocks.

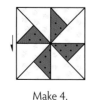

Make 4.

4. Sew two red B triangles to one cream C triangle as shown to make a flying-geese unit. Press the seam allowances toward the red triangles. Repeat to make a total of 16 flying-geese units.

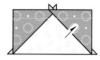

Make 16.

5. Sew two flying-geese units to opposite edges of one Windmill block as shown. Press the seam allowances toward the flying-geese units.

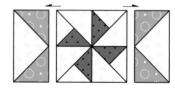

6. Sew cream 2¾" squares to opposite edges of two flying-geese units. Press the seam allowances toward the squares.

7. Sew the flying-geese units to the top and bottom edges of the Windmill block. Press the seam allowances toward the flying-geese units. Repeat to make a total of four large Martha Washington Star blocks. Set aside.

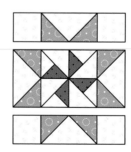
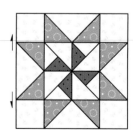

Make 4.

8. To assemble the small Martha Washington Star blocks, follow steps 1–7 using the cream D and red D triangles in step 1, the cream F triangles in step 2, the

★ ★ ★

10

cream E and blue F triangles in step 4, and the cream 2" squares in step 6. Note the change of color from blue to red in the Windmill block. Make a total of four small Martha Washington Star blocks.

MAKING THE FRIENDSHIP STAR BLOCKS

1. With right sides together, align one blue 2⅞" square with one beige 2⅞" square. On the beige square draw a diagonal line from corner to corner. Sew ¼" from each side of the drawn line. Cut on the drawn line to make two half-square-triangle units. Press the seam allowances toward the blue triangles. Repeat to make a total of 64 blue-and-beige half-square-triangle units.

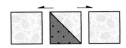

Make 64.

2. Sew two beige 2½" squares to one half-square-triangle unit, noting the position of the blue triangle, to make a top or bottom row. Press the seam allowances toward the beige square. Repeat to make a total of 32 rows.

   For the middle row, sew two half-square-triangle units to opposite sides of one blue 2½" square, again noting position of the blue triangles. Press the seam allowances toward the blue square. Repeat to make a total of 16 middle rows.

Make 32.   Make 16.

3. To assemble the block, sew the top and bottom rows to the middle row, paying close attention to the position of the half-square triangles. Press the seam allowances away from the middle row. Repeat to make a total of 16 Friendship Star blocks.

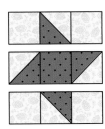

Make 16.

ASSEMBLING THE QUILT TOP

Press all seam allowances open unless otherwise instructed.

1. Join four large Martha Washington Star blocks in pairs; press. Join the pairs to make the center unit; press.

2. Join three Friendship Star blocks to make a short inner border; press. Repeat to make a second short inner border. Sew the border units to opposite sides of the center unit. Press the seam allowances toward the inner border. Join five Friendship Star blocks to make a long inner border; press. Repeat to make a second long inner border. Sew the border units to the top and bottom of the center unit. Press the seam allowances toward the inner border.

3. Match the center of one red 1" x 42" middle-border strip with the center of one side of the quilt top; sew the strip to the quilt top with right sides together. Repeat to sew a second red 1" x 42" strip to the opposite side of the quilt top. Press the seam allowances toward the middle border. Trim the ends even with the quilt top. Sew the remaining red 1" x 42" strips to the top and bottom of the quilt top. Press the seam allowances toward the middle border. Trim the ends as before.

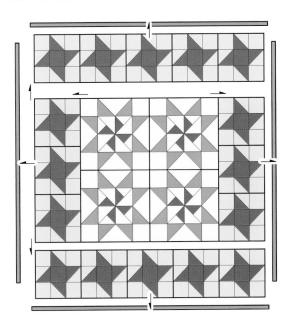

★　★　★

4. For the piano-key outer border, sew one red 1⅞" x 42" strip to each cream 1¾" x 42" strip to make four red-and-cream strip units. Sew one red 1¾" x 42" strip to each beige 1¾" x 42" strip to make four red-and-beige strip units. Crosscut each strip unit into six sections, 6½" wide.

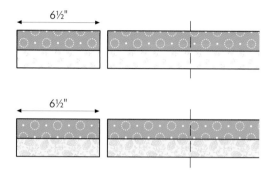

5. Sew 12 alternating red-and-cream and red-and-beige sections along the long edges to make a short outer border. Repeat to make a total of four short outer borders. If needed, trim the ends even with the quilt top. Sew two short outer borders to the sides of the quilt top. Press the seam allowances toward the outer borders.

6. Sew one small Martha Washington Star block to each end of the remaining short outer borders to make long outer borders as shown in the assembly diagram below. Press the seam allowances toward the center. Sew the long outer borders to the top and bottom of the quilt top. Press the seam allowances toward the middle border.

FINISHING THE QUILT

For more information on any of the following steps, refer to "Quiltmaking Basics" on page 56. You also can download free illustrated instructions about finishing your quilt at ShopMartingale.com/HowtoQuilt.

1. Layer and baste the quilt top, batting, and backing.

2. Quilt as desired. The sample is quilted with meandering wavy lines and star shapes.

3. Trim the backing and batting even with the quilt top.

4. Using the red 2½"-wide strips, make and attach the binding to finish the edges of the quilt.

★ ★ ★

Stars of Freedom

A great project for using up your scraps, this little table topper can be as scrappy or fabric-coordinated as you choose. Use the six-pointed star to practice your hand-piecing skills, or piece it by machine. Either method will be sure to boost your confidence with Y-seams.

"Stars of Freedom," designed by Jo Beth Simons

FINISHED QUILT: 21½" x 24"

MATERIALS

Yardage is based on 42"-wide fabric.

1⅛ yards of muslin for blocks and backing

½ yard *total* of assorted red prints for star points and binding*

½ yard *total* of assorted blue prints for star points and binding*

⅓ yards *total* of assorted cream-red-and-blue prints for star points*

28" x 30" piece of batting

Template plastic

*If you prefer to use scraps for your stars, a 3" x 15" piece of fabric will yield 3 star points. See "Cutting the Star Points," step 2, for the total number of star points needed from each fabric. Two stars in the original quilt contain fabrics that vary slightly from what is listed; the materials and cutting lists have been simplified for ease of construction.

CUTTING

From the muslin, cut:

1 rectangle, 36" x 42"; cut into 3 strips as shown: 9" x 42", 10" x 27", and 27" x 32"

    From the 9" x 42" strip, cut 3 strips, 3" x 42"

    From the 10" x 27" strip, cut 2 strips, 3" x 10"

Set aside the 27" x 32" strip for the backing.

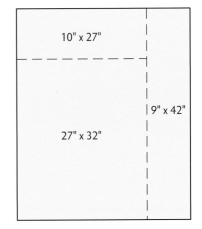

Cutting diagram

Continued on page 15

Continued from page 13

From the assorted red prints, cut:

3 strips, 3" x 42"

2 strips, 2½" x 42"

From the assorted blue prints, cut:

3 strips, 3" x 42"

2 strips, 2½" x 42"

From the assorted cream-red-and-blue prints, cut:

3 strips, 3" x 42"

CUTTING THE STAR POINTS

1. Trace the star-point template pattern on page 16 onto template plastic, including the straight of grain arrow. If you're hand piecing this project, trace using the inside lines of the pattern. If machine piecing, trace using the outside lines. Cut out the template.

2. Using the muslin 3" x 42" and 3" x 10" strips, the assorted 3" x 42" strips, and the star-point template, align the marked arrow on the template with the straight of grain in each fabric strip. Cut a total of 29 muslin star points, 30 *each* of red and blue star points, and 24 cream-red-and-blue star points.

ASSEMBLING THE QUILT TOP

See "Tip for Sewing Y-Seams" at right.

1. Place a dot ¼" in from each star point. With right sides together, align one red and one blue star point, matching dots; pin. Sew between the dots, backstitching a few stitches at the beginning and end of the seam. Press the seam allowances toward the blue star point. In the same manner, add a second red star point to the blue star point to yield a red-blue-red star point unit. Repeat to make a total of 6 red-blue-red star-point units.

Make 6.

2. Changing the position of the red and blue star points, repeat step 1 to make a total of 6 blue-red-blue star-point units.

3. Align one red-blue-red star unit with one blue-red-blue unit to make a red-blue six-pointed star. Repeat to make a total of six red-blue six-pointed stars.

Make 6.

4. Using 12 cream-red-and-blue and 12 blue star points, repeat steps 1–3 to make a total of four cream-and-blue six-pointed stars. Using 12 cream-red-and-blue and 12 red star points, repeat steps 1–3 to make a total of four cream-and-red six-pointed stars.

> **Tip for Sewing Y-Seams** ★ ★ ★ ★ ★
>
> The secret to sewing Y-seams is knowing where to start and stop stitching. Y-seams are nothing more than mitered corners but on a smaller scale. Simply stated, you start and stop stitching ¼" in from each edge of the piece you're working on. Mark a dot ¼" in on each edge. Stitch slowly between the dots, take a few backstitches, and press the seam allowances carefully so they lie flat. Repeat until you're comfortable with the technique.

5. Lay out the six-pointed stars and muslin star points in five rows as shown on page 16. Sew together the pieces in the six-pointed-star rows first. Press the seam allowances toward the six-pointed stars.

Add the muslin star points to the just-sewn rows as shown; press. Then join rows 1–5 and press to complete the quilt top.

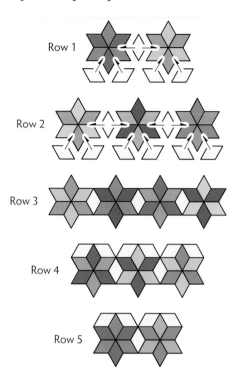

Row 1

Row 2

Row 3

Row 4

Row 5

6. Trim the star points so they are even with the edge of the Star blocks as shown.

FINISHING THE QUILT

For more information on any of the following steps, refer to "Quiltmaking Basics" on page 56. You also can download free illustrated instructions about finishing your quilt at ShopMartingale.com/HowtoQuilt.

1. Layer and baste the quilt top, batting, and 27" x 32" muslin backing.

2. Quilt as desired. The sample is echo-quilted ¼" inside each seamline.

3. Trim the backing and batting even with the quilt top.

4. Using the red and blue 2½"-wide strips, make and attach the binding to finish the edges of the quilt.

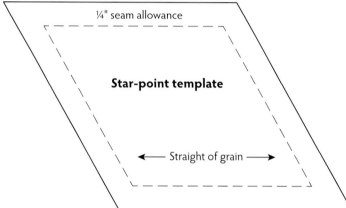

¼" seam allowance

Star-point template

← Straight of grain →

Leo's Star

The American flag is one of the most respected and recognizable symbols of our freedom. This simple-to-stitch quilted flag is one you can proudly display each day throughout the year to show support for the men and women in our military who give their unconditional service as they secure our freedom.

"Leo's Star," designed by Patty Winkler

FINISHED QUILT: 12½" x 14"

FINISHED BLOCK: 12" x 12"

★ ## MATERIALS

★ *Yardage is based on 42"-wide fabric. Fat quarters measure approximately 18" x 21". Fat eighths measure approximately 9" x 21".*

★ 1 fat quarter of dark-blue print for half-square triangles and binding

★ 1 fat eighth of red-white-and-blue print for half-square triangles and corner squares

★ 1 fat eighth of red print for top and bottom borders

★ 10" x 10" rectangle of red-and-white stripe for block center

★ 5" x 5" piece of dark-blue star print for block center

★ 19" x 20" piece of fabric for backing

★ 18" x 22" piece of batting

★ ## CUTTING

★ **From the dark-blue star print, cut:**
1 square, 3½" x 3½"

★ **From the red-and-white stripe, cut:**
1 rectangle, 3½" x 6½"
1 square, 3½" x 3½"

★ **From the red-white-and-blue print, cut:**
1 strip, 4" x 16"; crosscut into 4 squares, 4" x 4"
1 strip, 3½" x 16"; crosscut into 4 squares, 3½" x 3½"

★ **From the dark-blue print:**
1 strip, 4" x 21"; crosscut into 4 squares, 4" x 4"
4 strips, 2½" x 21"

★ **From the red print, cut:**
2 strips, 1¼" x 12½"

ASSEMBLING THE QUILT TOP

1. With right sides together, sew the star-print 3½"
   square to the red-and-white stripe 3½" square
   to make a blue-and-red unit. Press the seam
   allowances open. Sew the blue-and-red unit and
   the red-and-white 3½" x 6½" rectangle along the
   long edges to make the block center. Press the seam
   allowances open.

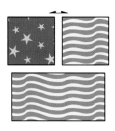 

2. Draw a diagonal line from corner to corner on the
   wrong side of a red-white-and-blue 4" square. With
   right sides together, lay the marked 4" square on
   a dark-blue 4" square. Sew ¼" from each side of
   the drawn line. Cut on the drawn line to make two
   half-square-triangle units. Press the seam allowances
   toward the dark-blue triangles. Trim the half-square-
   triangle units to 3½" square. Repeat to make a total of
   eight half-square-triangle units.

Make 8.

3. Sew together two half-square-triangle units to make
   a star-point unit; note the position of the dark-blue
   triangles. Press the seam allowances open. Repeat to
   make a total of four star-point units.

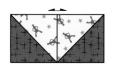

Make 4.

4. Sew a red-white-and-blue 3½" square to each end of
   two star-point units. Press the seam allowances open.

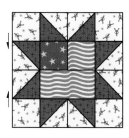

Make 2.

5. Sew the remaining two star-point units from step 3
   to opposite sides of the block center. Press the seam
   allowances toward the block center. Sew the star-
   point units from step 4 to the top and bottom edges
   to make the Star block. Press the seam allowances
   toward the block center.

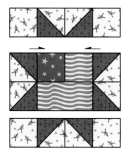

6. Square up the Star block to 12½", if needed. Sew
   one red 1¼"-wide border strip to the top of
   the Star block. Press the seam allowances toward the
   Star block. Repeat to add the red border to the
   bottom of the block.

FINISHING THE QUILT

For more information on any of the following steps,
refer to "Quiltmaking Basics" on page 56. You also can
download free illustrated instructions about finishing
your quilt at ShopMartingale.com/HowtoQuilt.

1. Layer and baste the quilt top, batting, and backing.

2. Quilt as desired. The sample is stitched in the ditch.

3. Trim the backing and batting even with the quilt top.
   Add a hanging sleeve, if desired. (You will need a
   2½" x 11" strip of coordinating fabric for a hanging
   sleeve. For more information about adding a hanging
   sleeve and a display hanger, see page 59.)

4. Using the dark-blue 2½"-wide strips, make and attach
   the binding to finish the edges of the quilt.

★ ★ ★

Stars and Stripes

Martha Washington was not only a strong patriotic woman but is also considered the mother of our country. We honor her with this sweet little table topper, which is easily put together in an afternoon. It's charming on a nightstand or end table.

"Stars and Stripes," designed by Kathy Flowers

FINISHED QUILT: 14" x 18½"

FINISHED BLOCK: 4½" x 4½"

MATERIALS

Yardage is based on 42"-wide fabric. Fat quarters measure approximately 18" x 21".

½ yard of blue print for blocks, border, and binding

½ yard of red-and-cream print for blocks and border

¼ yard of red print for blocks and border

1 fat quarter of fabric for backing

18" x 21" piece of batting

CUTTING

From the red-and-cream print, cut:

1 strip, 3½" x 42"; crosscut into 2 squares, 3½" x 3½"; cut the squares into quarters diagonally to yield 8 C triangles

1 strip, 2⅜" x 42"; crosscut into 4 squares, 2⅜" x 2⅜"; cut the squares into quarters diagonally to yield 16 A triangles

1 strip 2" x 42"; crosscut into 8 squares, 2" x 2"; cut the squares in half diagonally to yield 16 B triangles

1 strip 2" x 42"; crosscut into 2 strips, 2" x 18½"

1 strip, 1⅝" x 42"; crosscut into 8 squares, 1⅝" x 1⅝"

From the blue print, cut:

1 strip, 3½" x 42"; crosscut into 2 squares, 3½" x 3½"; cut the squares into quarters diagonally to yield 8 C triangles

1 strip, 2⅜" x 42"; crosscut into 4 squares, 2⅜" x 2⅜"; cut the squares into quarters diagonally to yield 16 A triangles

1 strip, 2" x 42"; crosscut into 2 strips, 2" x 18½"

1 strip, 1⅝" x 42"; crosscut into 8 squares, 1⅝" x 1⅝"

2 strips, 2½" x 42"

From the red print, cut:

1 strip, 2" x 42"; crosscut into 16 squares, 2" x 2"; cut the squares in half diagonally to yield 32 B triangles

1 strip, 2" x 42"; crosscut into 2 strips, 2" x 18½"

MAKING THE MARTHA WASHINGTON STAR BLOCKS

1. Align one red-and-cream A triangle atop one blue A triangle, right sides together. Join along one short edge to make a blue-and-cream triangle unit. Press the seam allowances toward the blue triangle. Repeat to make a total of 16 blue-and-cream triangle units, always placing the blue triangle on the bottom.

2. Align one red-and-cream B triangle with one blue-and-cream triangle unit. Sew along the long edge to make a windmill unit. Press the seam allowances toward the red-and-cream triangle. Repeat to make a total of 16 windmill units.

Make 16.

3. Lay out four windmill units as shown; join in pairs and press the seam allowances toward the blue triangle. Join the windmill unit pairs as shown to make a Windmill block. Press the seam allowances in one direction. Repeat to make a total of four Windmill blocks.

Make 4.

4. Sew two red B triangles to one blue C triangle as shown to make a flying-geese unit. Press the seam allowances toward the red triangles. Repeat to make a total of eight red-and-blue flying-geese units. Using 16 red B triangles and eight red-and-cream C triangles, repeat to make a total of eight red-and-cream flying geese units.

Make 8 red and blue.
Make 8 red and cream.

5. Sew two red-and-blue flying-geese units to opposite edges of one Windmill block. Press the seam allowances toward the flying-geese units.

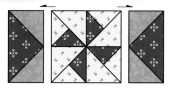

6. Sew blue 1⅝" squares to opposite edges of two red-and-blue flying-geese units. Press the seam allowances toward the squares.

Make 4.

7. Sew the flying-geese units from step 6 to the top and bottom edges of the Windmill block to make a red-and-blue Martha Washington Star block. Press the seam allowances toward the flying-geese units. Repeat to make a second red-and-blue Martha Washington Star block.

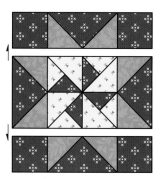

Make 2.

8. Using the remaining Windmill blocks, red-and-cream flying-geese units, and red-and-cream 1⅝" squares, repeat steps 5–7 to make two red-and-cream Martha Washington Star blocks.

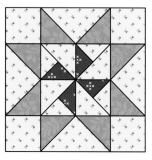

Make 2.

★ ★ ★

9. Sew the four blocks together, alternating the red-and-blue and red-and-cream blocks to make the quilt center. Press the seam allowances toward the red-and-blue blocks. Set aside.

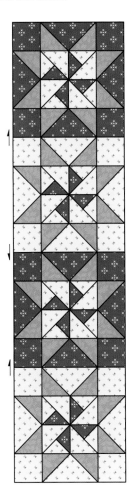

10. Sew together one *each* of the red, red-and-cream, and blue 2" x 18½" strips along the long edges to make a border unit as shown. Repeat to make a second border unit.

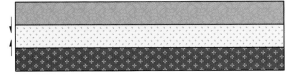

Make 2.

11. Match the center of one border unit with the quilt center along one long edge; pin. Sew the border unit to the quilt center. Press the seam allowances toward the border. Repeat to add the remaining border unit to the remaining long edge of the quilt center to complete the quilt top.

FINISHING THE QUILT

For more information on any of the following steps, refer to "Quiltmaking Basics" on page 56. You also can download free illustrated instructions about finishing your quilt at ShopMartingale.com/HowtoQuilt.

1. Layer and baste the quilt top, batting, and backing.

2. Quilt as desired. The sample is stitched in the ditch in the blocks. Double wavy lines accent the red strips in the borders. A straight line is stitched down the center of each red-and-cream strip, and diamond shapes are stitched in each blue strip.

3. Trim the backing and batting even with the quilt top.

4. Using the blue 2½"-wide strips, make and attach the binding to finish the edges of the quilt.

★ ★ ★

Pappa Bear

This queen-size quilt is sure to please the quilter who wants to put together something simple yet striking. Create 32 Bear Paw blocks accented with 31 simple Center Dot blocks that are easily chain-pieced for quick assembly.

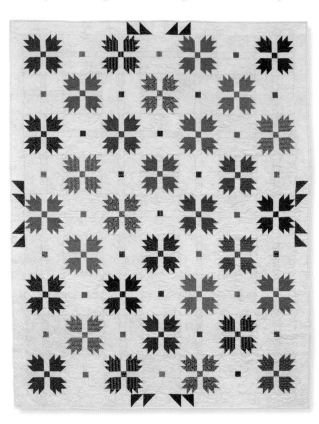

"Pappa Bear," designed by Kathy Flowers

FINISHED QUILT: 67¾" x 85¼"

FINISHED BLOCK: 8¾" x 8¾"

MATERIALS

Yardage is based on 42"-wide fabric. Yardage given is for one blue print throughout. For the quilt shown, I used a variety of 11 blue fat quarters from my stash, which works equally well. One fat quarter will yield enough pieces for 3 Bear Paw blocks and 3 Center Dot blocks.

6⅓ yards of mottled beige fabric for blocks and binding
2¼ yards of blue print for blocks
5⅓ yards of fabric for backing
77" x 95" piece of batting

CUTTING

From the mottled-beige fabric, cut:
16 strips, 4¼" x 42"; crosscut into 62 rectangles,
   4¼" x 9¼"
15 strips, 2⅛" x 42"; crosscut into 256 squares,
   2⅛" x 2⅛"
22 strips, 1¾" x 42"; crosscut into 190 rectangles,
   1¾" x 4¼"
6 strips, 1¾" x 42"; crosscut into 128 squares, 1¾" x 1¾"
1 strip, 3⅞" x 42"; crosscut into 8 squares, 3⅞" x 3⅞"
9 strips, 3½" x 42"; from 1 of the strips, cut 4 squares,
   3½" x 3½"
8 strips, 2½" x 42"

From the blue print, cut:
15 strips, 2⅛" x 42"; crosscut into 256 squares,
   2⅛" x 2⅛"
10 strips, 3" x 42"; crosscut into 128 squares, 3" x 3"
3 strips, 1¾" x 42"; crosscut into 63 squares, 1¾" x 1¾"
1 strip, 3⅞" x 42"; crosscut into 8 squares, 3⅞" x 3⅞"

MAKING THE BEAR PAW BLOCKS

1. Draw a diagonal line from corner to corner on the wrong side of a beige 2⅛" square. With right sides together, lay the marked 2⅛" square on a blue 2⅛" square. Sew ¼" from each side of the drawn line. Cut on the drawn line to make two half-square-triangle units. Press the seam allowances toward the blue triangles. Repeat to make a total of 512 half-square-triangle units.

Make 512.

2. With right sides together, sew two half-square-triangle units in pairs; note the position of the blue triangles. Press the seam allowances toward the blue triangles. Repeat to make a total of 256 pairs.

Make 256.

3. Sew one beige 1¾" square to the right side of a pair of units from step 2 to make a blue segment. Press the seam allowances toward the beige square. Repeat to make 128 blue segments.

Make 128.

4. Sew together a pair of units from step 2 and a blue 3" square. Press the seam allowances toward the blue square. Sew a blue segment from step 3 to an adjacent edge of the blue square as shown to make a bear paw unit. Press the seam allowances toward the blue square. Repeat to make a total of 128 bear paw units.

Make 128.

5. Sew together two bear paw units and one beige 1¾" x 4¼" rectangle along the long edges to make a bear paw strip. Press the seam allowances toward the beige rectangle. Repeat to make a total of 64 bear paw strips.

Make 64.

6. Sew together one blue 1¾" square and two beige 1¾" x 4¼" rectangles along the short edges to make a center strip. Press the seam allowances toward the beige strips. Repeat to make a total of 32 center strips.

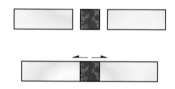

Make 32.

7. Sew together two bear paw strips and one center strip in three rows to make a Bear Paw block. Press the seam allowances toward the center strip. Repeat to make total of 32 Bear Paw blocks.

Make 32.

MAKING THE CENTER DOT BLOCKS

1. Sew together one blue 1¾" square and two beige 1¾" x 4¼" rectangles along the short edges to make a center strip. Press the seam allowances toward the blue square. Repeat to make a total of 31 center strips.

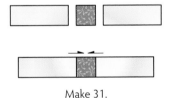

Make 31.

2. Sew together two beige 4¼" x 9¼" rectangles and a center strip from step 1 as shown to make a Center Dot block. Press the seam allowances toward the beige rectangles. Repeat to make a total of 31 Center Dot blocks.

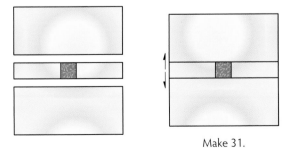

Make 31.

ASSEMBLING THE QUILT CENTER

Lay out Bear Paw blocks and Center Dot blocks in nine rows of seven blocks each, alternating blocks and rotating the Center Dot blocks 90° from one row to the next. Sew together the blocks in each row. Press the seam allowances toward the Center Dot blocks. Join the rows to make the quilt center; press the seam allowances in one direction.

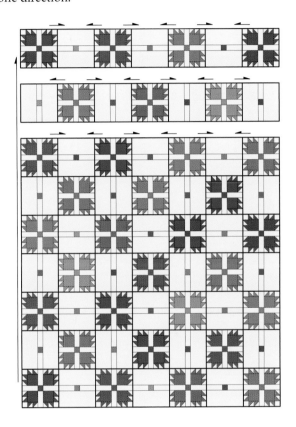

ADDING THE BORDERS

1. Draw a diagonal line from corner to corner on the wrong side of a beige 3⅞" square. With right sides together, lay the marked 3⅞" square on a blue 3⅞" square. Sew ¼" from each side of the drawn line. Cut on the drawn line to make two half-square-triangle units. Press the seam allowances toward the blue triangles. Repeat to make a total of 16 half-square-triangle units. Trim each to 3½" square.

Make 16.

2. Sew together four half-square-triangle units and one beige 3½" square to make a border unit. Press the seam allowances toward the beige square. Repeat to make a total of four border units.

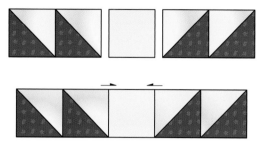

Make 4.

3. Sew a beige 3½" x 42" strip to each end of a border unit from step 2 to make a border strip. Press the seam allowances toward the beige strip. Repeat to make a total of four border strips.

4. Align one border strip from step 3 along one short edge of the quilt center, matching centers; sew together. Press the seam allowances toward the border strip. Repeat on the opposite edge. Trim the ends even with the quilt center. Repeat on the side edges with the remaining border strips, matching the centers and trimming the ends to complete the quilt top as shown in the assembly diagram below.

FINISHING THE QUILT

For more information on any of the following steps, refer to "Quiltmaking Basics" on page 56. You also can download free illustrated instructions about finishing your quilt at ShopMartingale.com/HowtoQuilt.

1. Layer and baste the quilt top, batting, and backing.

2. Quilt as desired. The sample is quilted with an allover design of loops and swirls.

3. Trim the backing and batting even with the quilt top.

4. Using the beige 2½"-wide strips, make and attach the binding to finish the edges of the quilt.

★ ★ ★

I Am Honored

Make a bold patriotic statement using this quilt as a wall hanging—or display it as a bed topper. Quick and easy to make, the pattern uses only five Ohio Star blocks and five long strip sets. The light small-scale stripe in the background fabric gives the illusion of a much longer quilt.

"I Am Honored," designed by Kathy Flowers

FINISHED QUILT: 39⅞" x 54⅞"

FINISHED BLOCK: 7⅞" x 7⅞"

★ **MATERIALS**

★ *Yardage is based on 42"-wide fabric.*

★ 2 yards of cream print for blocks and strip sets

★ 1 yard of blue print for strip sets and binding

★ ⅜ yard of red print for blocks

★ 2¾ yards of fabric for backing

★ 49" x 63" piece of batting

★ **CUTTING**

From the cream print, cut:
2 strips, 3⅞" x 42"; crosscut into 20 squares, 3⅞" x 3⅞"
2 strips, 3⅛" x 42"; crosscut into 20 squares, 3⅛" x 3⅛"
2 strips, 3" x 39½"
4 strips, 3" x 31⅝"
4 strips, 3" x 23¾"
4 strips, 8⅜" x 12½"
1 strip, 8" x 8⅜"

From the red print, cut:
2 strips, 3⅞" x 42"; crosscut into 20 squares, 3⅞" x 3⅞"
1 strip, 3⅛" x 42"; crosscut into 5 squares, 3⅛" x 3⅛"

From the blue print, cut:
5 strips, 2½" x 42"
1 strip, 3⅜" x 39½"
2 strips, 3⅜" x 31⅝"
2 strips, 3⅜" x 23¾"

MAKING THE OHIO STAR BLOCKS

1. Draw a line diagonally from corner to corner on the wrong side of a cream 3⅞" square. With right sides together, lay a marked 3⅞" square on a red 3⅞" square. Sew ¼" from each side of the drawn line. Cut on the drawn line to make two red-and-cream half-square-triangle units. Press the seam allowances toward the red triangle. Repeat to make a total of 40 red-and-cream half-square-triangle units.

Make 40.

2. Place two red-and-cream half-square triangles right sides together, with the red print over the cream print, nesting the seams. Using the same method as in step 1, draw a line perpendicular to the seamline and sew ¼" from each side of the drawn line. Cut on the drawn line. Press the seam allowances in one direction to make two hourglass squares. Trim each hourglass square to 3⅛" square. Repeat to make a total of 20 hourglass squares.

Make 20.

3. Sew two cream 3⅛" squares to opposite edges of an hourglass square, noting the position of the red triangles, to make a top row. Press the seam allowances toward the cream squares. Repeat to make a bottom row.

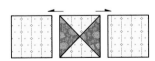

4. Sew two hourglass squares to opposite edges of one red 3⅛" square, again noting position of the red triangles, to make the middle row. Press the seam allowances toward the red square.

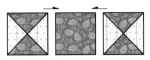

5. Sew the top and bottom rows to the middle row to make an Ohio Star block. Press the seam allowances away from the middle row.

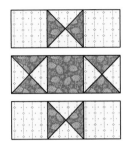 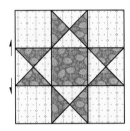

Make 5.

6. Repeat steps 3–5 to make a total of five Ohio Star blocks.

ASSEMBLING THE QUILT TOP

1. With right sides together, sew two cream 3" x 23¾" strips and one blue print 3⅜" x 23¾" strip along the long edges to make a short strip set. Press the seam allowances toward the blue strip. Repeat to make a second short strip set.

2. Repeat step 1 using four cream 3" x 31⅝" strips and two blue 3⅜" x 31⅝" strips to make two medium-length strip sets. Repeat step 1 using two cream 3" x 39½" strips and one blue 3⅜" x 39½" strip to make a long strip set.

3. Sew an Ohio Star block to one end of each strip set to make five pieced rows. Press the seam allowances toward the strip set.

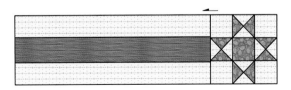

4. Measure and mark 4" from the right-hand end of two cream 8⅜" x 12½" strips. Using an acrylic ruler and a rotary cutter and mat, position the ruler on one cream strip, aligning the 45° angle with the horizontal edge of the strip. Cut a 45° angle from the bottom edge to the top edge at the 4" mark as shown. Repeat with the second strip.

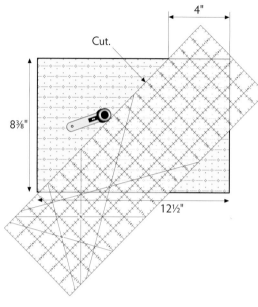

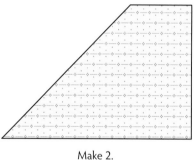

Make 2.

5. Repeat step 4, measuring and marking 4" from the left-hand end of two cream 8⅜" x 12½" strips and cutting the 45° angle in a reverse direction as shown.

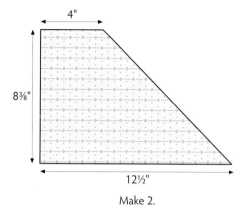

Make 2.

6. Fold the cream 8" x 8⅜" strip in half lengthwise; the folded strip should measure 4³⁄₁₆" x 8". Lightly finger-press the fold to crease the centerline. Unfold. Referring to the method used in step 4, cut the 45° angle in both directions at one end of the cream 8" x 8⅜" strip as shown, using the centerline as a guide for creating the point.

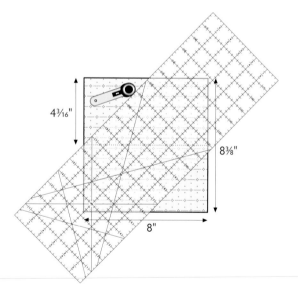

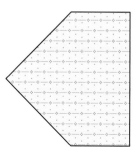

7. Lay out the pieced rows from step 3 and the angled cream strips from steps 4–6 as shown below, noting the direction of the cut angles on the strip ends. Sew together the pieced rows and angled strips. Press the seam allowances toward the angled cream strips. Join rows 1–5 to complete the quilt top. Press the seam allowances open.

FINISHING THE QUILT

For more information on any of the following steps, refer to "Quiltmaking Basics" on page 56. You also can download free illustrated instructions about finishing your quilt at ShopMartingale.com/HowtoQuilt.

1. Layer and baste the quilt top, batting, and backing.

2. Quilt as desired. The sample is stipple quilted around star shapes in the cream background. An orange-peel design encircles the Ohio Star blocks.

3. Trim the backing and batting even with the quilt top.

4. Using the blue 2½"-wide strips, make and attach the binding to finish the edges of the quilt.

★ ★ ★

Long May She Wave

Four stars and alternating red and white Courthouse Steps blocks strategically placed and rotated create a vision of our pride, the American flag, perfect for a wall hanging or back-of-sofa lap quilt.

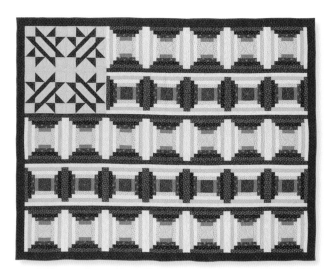

"Long May She Wave," designed by Kathy Flowers

FINISHED QUILT: 61" x 78"

FINISHED BLOCKS:
Courthouse Steps: 10½" x 10½"
Stars: 10½" x 10½"

MATERIALS

Yardage is based on 42"-wide fabric. In the featured quilt, I used 6 red prints and 5 shirting fabrics or light prints.

2¼ yards of red print #1 for Star blocks, sashing, borders, and binding

⅓ yard of red print #2 for Courthouse Steps block centers

⅜ yard of red print #3 for Courthouse Steps blocks

⅝ yard *each* of red prints #4 and #5 for Courthouse Steps blocks

¾ yard of red print #6 for Courthouse Steps blocks

1 yard of shirting #1 for Courthouse Steps block centers and Star blocks

⅝ yard *each* of shirting #2 and #3 for Courthouse Steps blocks

¾ yard of shirting #4 for Courthouse Steps blocks

1 yard of shirting #5 for Courthouse Steps blocks

5 yards of fabric for backing

69" x 86" piece of batting

CUTTING

From red print #1, cut:

2 strips, 3½" x 42"; crosscut into 16 squares, 3½" x 3½"; cut the squares in half diagonally to yield 32 A triangles

16 strips, 2½" x 42"

8 strips, 1½" x 42"

8 strips, 1½" x 6⅞"

From red print #2, cut:

2 strips, 4" x 42"; crosscut into 12 squares, 4" x 4"

From red print #3, cut:

7 strips, 1⅜" x 42"; crosscut into 62 strips, 1⅜" x 4"

From red print #4, cut:

11 strips, 1⅜" x 42"; crosscut into 62 strips, 1⅜" x 5¾"

From red print #5, cut:

13 strips, 1⅜" x 42"; crosscut into 62 strips, 1⅜" x 7½"

From red print #6, cut:

16 strips, 1⅜" x 42"; crosscut into 62 strips, 1⅜" x 9¼"

Continued on page 36

★ ★ ★

34

Continued from page 34

From shirting #1, cut:

1 strip, 6¾" x 42"; crosscut into 4 squares, 6¾" x 6¾";
  cut the squares into quarters diagonally to yield 16 B triangles

2 strips, 4" x 42"; crosscut into 19 squares, 4" x 4"

1 strip, 3½" x 42"; crosscut into 4 squares, 3½" x 3½"; cut the squares in half diagonally to yield 8 A triangles

2 strips, 3⅛" x 42"; crosscut into 16 squares, 3⅛" x 3⅛"

1 strip, 2¼" x 42"; crosscut into 4 strips, 2¼" x 9"

1 strip, 1½" x 21½"

From shirting #2, cut:

11 strips, 1⅜" x 42"; crosscut into 62 strips, 1⅜" x 5¾"

From shirting #3, cut:

13 strips, 1⅜" x 42"; crosscut into 62 strips, 1⅜" x 7½"

From shirting #4, cut:

16 strips, 1⅜" x 42"; crosscut into 62 strips, 1⅜" x 9¼"

From shirting #5, cut:

21 strips, 1⅜" x 42"; crosscut into 62 strips, 1⅜" x 11"

MAKING THE COURTHOUSE STEPS BLOCKS

1. With right sides together, sew two 1⅜" x 4" red #3 strips to opposite edges of one 4" red #2 square. Press the seam allowances toward the strips.

2. Sew two 1⅜" x 5¾" shirting #2 strips to the remaining edges of the unit from step 1. Press the seam allowances toward the just-added strips.

3. Continue in the same manner, adding strips and alternating between the red print and shirting to make a red Courthouse Steps block. Press all the seam allowances toward the strips just added. Repeat

to make a total of 12 red Courthouse Steps blocks. The blocks should measure 11", including seam allowances.

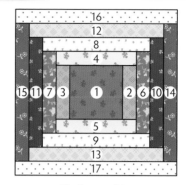

Block assembly.
Make 12.

4. Repeat step 1, starting with one 4" shirting #1 square and two 1⅜" x 4" red #3 strips. Repeat steps 2 and 3, using two 1⅜" x 5¾" shirting #2 strips, and then continuing to add strips and alternating between the red print and shirting to make a total of 19 white Courthouse Steps blocks.

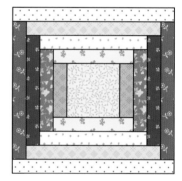

Block assembly.
Make 19.

MAKING THE STAR BLOCKS

1. Using an acrylic ruler and a rotary cutter and mat, position the ruler on one 1½" x 6⅞" red #1 strip, aligning the 45° angle with the horizontal edge of the strip, to cut a 45° angle on both ends. Note the direction of the angles on each end of the strip.

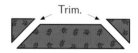

Trim.

2. With right side together, match the center of one shirting #1 A triangle with the center of the strip from step 1 and sew together to make a unit. Press the seam allowances toward the red strip. Repeat to make a second unit.

3. Sew the two units from step 2 centered on opposite edges of the 2¼" x 9" shirting #1 strip to make a unit. Press the seam allowances toward the red rectangles. Trim the unit as shown to make a 5¾" block center.

 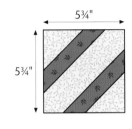

4. Sew two red #1 A triangles to the short edges of a shirting #1 B triangle to make a flying-geese unit. Press the seam allowances toward the red triangles. Repeat to make a total of four flying-geese units that measure 3⅛" x 5¾".

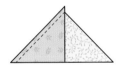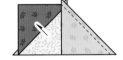

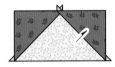

Make 4.

5. Sew two 3⅛" shirting #1 squares to opposite edges of a flying-geese unit to make a top block row. Press the seam allowances toward the squares. Repeat to make a bottom block row.

6. Sew two flying-geese units to the block center from step 3 to make a middle block row. Press the seam allowances toward the block center.

7. Sew the top and bottom block rows on opposite edges of the middle block row to make a Star block. Press the seam allowances toward the top and bottom rows. The block should measure 11" including seam allowances.

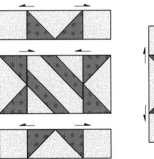 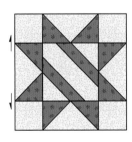

8. Repeat steps 1–7 to make a total of four Star blocks.

9. Sew together the Star blocks in pairs, noting the rotation of the blocks. Press the seam allowances open. Sew the 1½" x 21½" shirting #1 sashing strip to the bottom edge of one pair of Star blocks to make a star unit. Press the seam allowances toward the sashing strip.

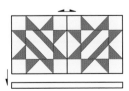

★   ★   ★

37

10. Join five white Courthouse Steps blocks as shown, noting the rotation of the blocks so the red strips are at the top and bottom. Press the seam allowances open. Piece and sew two 1½" x 42" red #1 sashing strips to the bottom edge of the joined blocks to make a block unit. Trim the ends even with the block unit. Press the seam allowances toward the sashing.

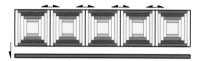

11. Sew together the star unit and the block unit to make row 1. Press the seam allowances open.

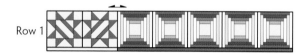

Row 1

12. Sew together the remaining two Star blocks, noting the rotation of the blocks. Sew together five red Courthouse Steps blocks so that the red strips are on the sides. Press the seam allowances open. Piece and sew two 1½" x 42" red #1 sashing strips to the bottom of the joined blocks to make row 2. Trim the ends even with the row. Press the seam allowances toward the sashing.

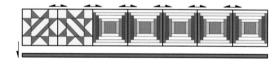

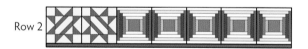

Row 2

13. Sew together seven white Courthouse Steps blocks so that the red strips are at the top and bottom to make row 3 and row 5. Piece and sew two 1½" x 42" red #1 sashing strips to the bottom of row 3. Trim the ends even with the row. Press the seam allowances toward the sashing.

Sew together seven red Courthouse Steps blocks so that the red strips are on the sides to make row 4. Piece and sew two 1½" x 42" red #1 sashing strips to

the bottom of the row. Trim the ends even with the row. Press the seam allowances toward the sashing.

Sew together rows 1–5 to make the quilt center. Press the seam allowances in one direction.

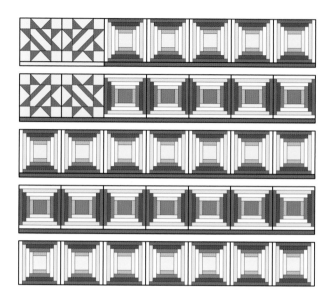

14. Sew together two 2½" x 42" red #1 strips at the short ends to make a short border strip. Repeat to make a second short border strip. Center a short border strip on each side of the quilt center and sew them to the quilt center. Press the seam allowances toward the border. Trim the ends even with the quilt top. Repeat to make two long border strips. Sew the long border strips to the top and bottom of the quilt center, trim, and press to complete the quilt top.

FINISHING THE QUILT

For more information on any of the following steps, refer to "Quiltmaking Basics" on page 56. You also can download free illustrated instructions about finishing your quilt at ShopMartingale.com/HowtoQuilt.

1. Layer and baste the quilt top, batting, and backing.

2. Quilt as desired. The sample is quilted with an allover meandering design around petal shapes in the centers of the Courthouse Steps blocks. The Star blocks feature petal shapes combined with an orange-peel design.

3. Trim the backing and batting even with the quilt top.

4. Using the remaining 2½"-wide red #1 strips, make and attach the binding to finish the edges of the quilt.

★ ★ ★

Americana Coasters

Calling all paper piecers! These little Log Cabin coasters are stash busters for sure. So easy to make! Not only are they fun, they make great hostess gifts or stocking stuffers for the holidays. Sew up a batch of these to keep on hand, and you'll always have a cute little gift with the homemade touch to pass around.

"Americana Coasters," designed by Kathy Flowers

FINISHED COASTER: 4" x 4"

★ **MATERIALS FOR 1 COASTER**

Scraps of cream, blue, and red prints for Log Cabin block
4½" square of coordinating print for backing
Add-A-Quarter Ruler (optional)

★ **CUTTING**

The following instructions are for one Log Cabin paper-pieced block. Repeat to make four blocks as shown in the photo.

From the cream prints, cut:
10 strips, 1" x 4½"

From the blue prints, cut:
5 strips, 1" x 4½"

From the red prints, cut:
5 strips, 1" x 4½"
1 square, 1¼" x 1¼"

Choosing a Dominant Color ★ ★ ★ ★ ★

My coasters are more cream than blue. Determine your dominant color and lay out your fabric strips accordingly. For example, to use cream as the dominant color, lay out the strips as follows (see the Log Cabin pattern on page 42):

Cream: strips 2, 3, 6, 7, 10, 11, 14, 15, 18, and 19

Blue: strips 4, 8, 12, 16, and 20

Red: square 1 and strips 5, 9, 13, 17, and 21

PAPER PIECING
THE LOG CABIN BLOCK

Before you begin to sew, set your sewing machine to a short stitch (18 to 20 stitches per inch). Make four copies of the Log Cabin block template pattern on page 42.

For more information on paper piecing, refer to "Paper Foundation Piecing" on page 61. You also can download free illustrated instructions about paper piecing at ShopMartingale.com/HowtoQuilt.

1. Position a red 1¼" square, right side up, on the *unprinted* side of the Log Cabin block template over the center square 1. Hold the template up to the light to make sure the fabric covers the stitch line ¼" between the pieces marked 1 and 2 on the template, as well as the outer ¼" seam allowances. Use a glue stick or pin to hold the fabric securely in place.

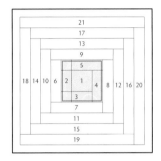

2. With right side down (so fabric right sides are together), place a cream strip over piece 2. Check that the strip covers the lines around piece 1 by pinning along the stitching line and folding the strip over the piece marked 1 on the template. Hold it up to the light to make sure the appropriate piece including all ¼" seam allowances are covered. If not, reposition the fabric. Once you're happy with the fabric placement, pin the layers in place with fabrics right sides together, and then flip over the template and fabric layers so the printed side of the template is *up*. On the *printed* side of the template, stitch on the line between pieces 1 and 2.

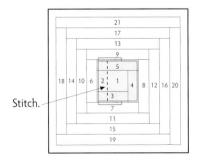

Stitch.

3. Fold the paper back along the stitched line and trim the excess fabric to ¼". (I use the Add-A-Quarter ruler made specifically for measuring and trimming accurate ¼" seam allowances.)

4. Press the fabrics open before positioning the next strip of fabric.

5. Place the next cream strip over pieces 1 and 2, right sides together, so that when it is pressed open it will cover all the lines around piece 3. To check placement, again pin your strip along the stitching line, fold the strip over piece 3, and hold it up to the light to make sure the appropriate piece including all ¼" seam allowances are covered. If not, reposition the fabric. Once you're happy with the fabric placement, pin the strip in place right sides together again, and then flip over the template and fabric layers so the printed side of the template is *up*. On the *printed* side of the template, stitch on the line that separates piece 3 from pieces 1 and 2.

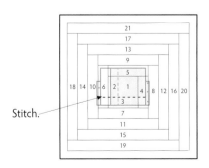

Stitch.

★　★　★

6. Continue in the same manner, repeating steps 2–4 using blue, red, and cream strips to cover the remaining pieces 4–21.

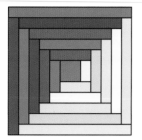

7. Trim the paper-pieced square along the outer dotted line on the printed side of the template. Carefully fold back the paper along the sewn lines and tear away the paper from the fabric (similar to tearing a check out of a checkbook) to make the Log Cabin block. Carefully press the block.

8. With right sides together, align the pieced block atop a coordinating-print 4½" square. Sew around the block using a ¼" seam allowance, leaving a small opening to turn the block inside out. Snip the corners, being careful not to cut through the stitching. Turn the block inside out and press. Whipstitch the small opening closed to complete the coaster.

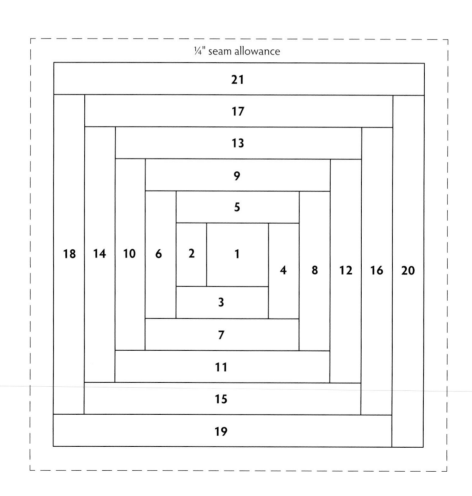

★ ★ ★

Eldorado

Create a small table topper for display with this easy paper-pieced project. Six Hummingbird blocks in red and blue surrounded by cream setting triangles make this a quick weekend quilt.

"Eldorado," designed by Kathy Flowers

FINISHED QUILT: 17½" x 26"

FINISHED BLOCK: 6" x 6"

MATERIALS

Yardage is based on 42"-wide fabric.

1 yard of cream print for setting triangles, paper-pieced blocks, and binding

⅛ yard *each* of 3 blue small-scale prints for paper-pieced blocks

⅛ yard *each* of 3 red small-scale prints for paper-pieced blocks

10" x 10" square of blue print for center square

10" x 10" square of red print for center square

¾ yard of fabric for backing

24" x 33" piece of batting

Add-A-Quarter Ruler (optional)

CUTTING

From *each* blue small-scale print, cut:
1 strip, 3" x 42"; crosscut into 4 squares, 3" x 3" (12 total)

From the cream print, cut:
4 strips, 3¾" x 42"; crosscut into 48 rectangles, 3¾" x 3"

1 strip, 9¾" x 42"; crosscut into 2 squares, 9¾" x 9¾"; cut each square into quarters diagonally to yield 8 A triangles (2 triangles will be extra)

2 squares, 5⅛" x 5⅛"; cut the squares in half diagonally to yield 4 B triangles

3 strips, 2½" x 42"

From *each* red small-scale print, cut:
1 strip, 3" x 42"; crosscut into 4 squares, 3" x 3" (12 total)

From the red print, cut:
1 square, 6½" x 6½"

From the blue print, cut:
1 square, 6½" x 6½"

PAPER PIECING THE HUMMINGBIRD BLOCKS

Before you sew, set your sewing machine to a short stitch length (18 to 20 stitches per inch). Make 24 copies of the Hummingbird block template pattern on page 47.

For more information on paper piecing, refer to "Paper Foundation Piecing" on page 61. You also can download free illustrated instructions about paper piecing at ShopMartingale.com/HowtoQuilt.

1. Position a blue 3" square, right side up, on the *unprinted* side of the Hummingbird block template over the piece marked 1 on the template. Hold the template up to a light to make sure the fabric covers the stitch line by ¼" between pieces 1 and 2, as well as the outer ¼" seam allowances. Use a glue stick or pin to hold the fabric securely in place.

2. With right side down (so the fabric right sides are together), place a cream 3¾" x 3" rectangle atop the blue square. Check that the rectangle covers the lines around piece 2 by pinning along the stitching line and folding the rectangle over the area marked 2 on the template. Hold it up to the light to make sure the appropriate area including all ¼" seam allowances are covered. If not, reposition the fabric. Once you're happy with the fabric placement, pin the layers in place with fabrics right sides together, and then flip over the template and fabric layers so the printed side of the template is *up*. On the *printed* side of the template, stitch on the line between pieces 1 and 2.

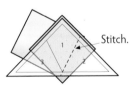

3. Fold the template back along the stitch line between pieces 1 and 2 and trim the excess fabric to ¼". (I use the Add-A-Quarter ruler made specifically for measuring and trimming accurate ¼" seam allowances.)

4. Press the fabrics open before positioning the next fabric rectangle.

5. Place the next cream 3¾" x 3" rectangle in place. Sew on the line between pieces 1 and 3. Trim and press the fabric open as before to make one quadrant.

Make 4.

6. Continue in the same manner, repeating steps 1–5 to make a total of four quadrants.

7. Trim the four paper-pieced quadrants along the outer dotted lines on the printed side of the template. Carefully fold back the paper along the sewn lines and tear away the paper from the fabric pieces. Carefully press each quadrant.

8. Lay out the four quadrants in pairs as shown. Sew together the pairs into half-blocks. Press the seam allowances open. Join the half blocks to make a blue Hummingbird block. Press the seam allowances open.

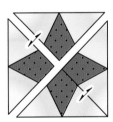 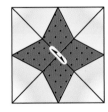

9. Repeat steps 1–8 to make a total of three blue Hummingbird blocks. Using the red 3" squares instead of the blue 3" squares, repeat steps 1–8 to make a total of three red Hummingbird blocks.

ASSEMBLING THE QUILT TOP

1. Sew two cream A triangles to opposite edges of one red Hummingbird block to make row 1 as shown in the assembly diagram below. Press the seam allowances toward the cream triangles.

2. Sew one blue Hummingbird block on opposite edges of the red 6½" square. Press the seam allowances toward the red square. Sew one cream A triangle on the left edge to make row 2. Wait until step 5 to add the cream B triangle. Press the seam allowances toward the cream triangle.

3. Sew two red Hummingbird blocks on opposite edges of the blue 6½" square. Press the seam allowances toward the blue square. Sew one cream A triangle on the right edge to make row 3. Wait until step 5 to add the cream B triangle. Press the seam allowances toward the cream triangle.

4. Sew two cream A triangles to opposite edges of the remaining blue Hummingbird block to make row 4. Press the seam allowances toward the cream triangles.

5. Sew the rows together, pressing the seam allowances open. Sew one cream B triangle to each corner to complete the quilt top. Press the seam allowances toward the corner triangles.

FINISHING THE QUILT

For more information on any of the following steps, refer to "Quiltmaking Basics" on page 56. You also can download free illustrated instructions about finishing your quilt at ShopMartingale.com/HowtoQuilt.

1. Layer and baste the quilt top, batting, and backing.

2. Quilt as desired. The sample is quilted with stippling in the Hummingbird blocks, a swirly fan motif in the center squares, and a swirly fan motif radiating from a half circle in the setting triangles. Parallel lines accent the corner triangles.

3. Trim the backing and batting even with the quilt top.

4. Using the cream 2½"-wide strips, make and attach the binding to finish the edges of the quilt.

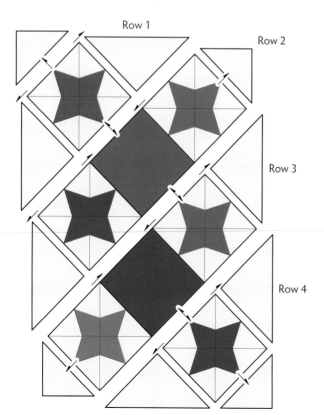

Row 1

Row 2

Row 3

Row 4

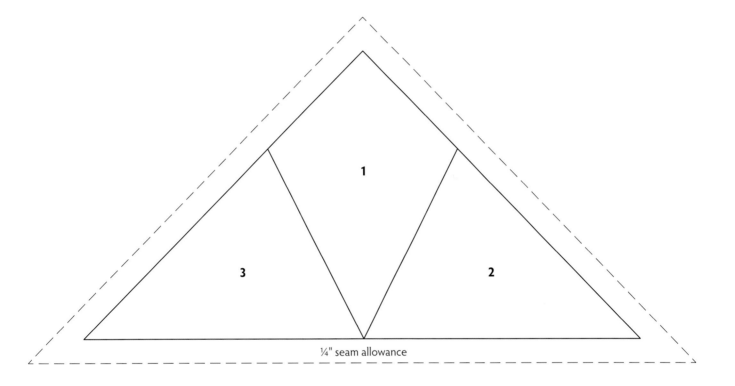

¼" seam allowance

Salute

Add patriotic charm to any room in the house with an easy-to-make Nine-Patch flag replica accented with three appliquéd wool stars. Simply leave it lying flat on a table or add a hanging sleeve to the quilt back to display it on an Ackfeld hanger.

"Salute," designed by Kathy Flowers

FINISHED QUILT: 11¾" x 14⅞"

FINISHED BLOCK: 4⅛" x 4⅛"

★ MATERIALS

Yardage is based on 42"-wide fabric. Fat quarters measure approximately 18" x 21". Fat eighths measure approximately 9" x 21".

1 fat eighth of cream small-scale print for blocks

1 fat eighth of red small-scale print for blocks and sashing squares

1 fat eighth of blue small-scale print for sashing

8" x 8" of gold felted wool for star appliqués

¼ yard of red-and-white diagonal stripe for binding

1 fat quarter of fabric for backing

18" x 21" piece of batting

Paper-backed fusible web for wool star appliqués

Optional: Ackfeld hanger (see page 59)

CUTTING

From the cream small-scale print, cut:

3 strips, 1⅞" x 21"

From the red small-scale print, cut:

3 strips, 1⅞" x 21"

1 strip, 1½" x 21"; crosscut into 4 squares, 1½" x 1½"

From the blue small-scale print, cut:

3 strips, 1½" x 21"; crosscut into 10 pieces, 1½" x 4⅝"

1 strip, 1½" x 21"; crosscut into 1 strip, 1½" x 14⅞"

From the red-and-white diagonal stripe, cut:

2 strips, 2½" x 42"

MAKING THE NINE PATCH BLOCKS

1. With right sides together, sew two cream 1⅞" x 21" strips and one red 1⅞" x 21" strip along the long edges as shown to make one strip set 1. Press the seam allowances toward the red strip. Cut into eight segments, 1⅞" wide. Repeat, using two red 1⅞" x 21" strips and one cream 1⅞" x 21" strip to make one strip set 2. Cut into 10 segments, 1⅞" wide.

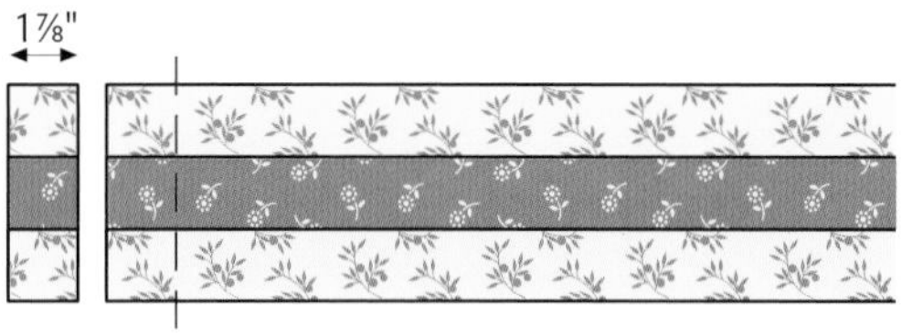

Strip set 1.
Make 1. Cut 8 segments.

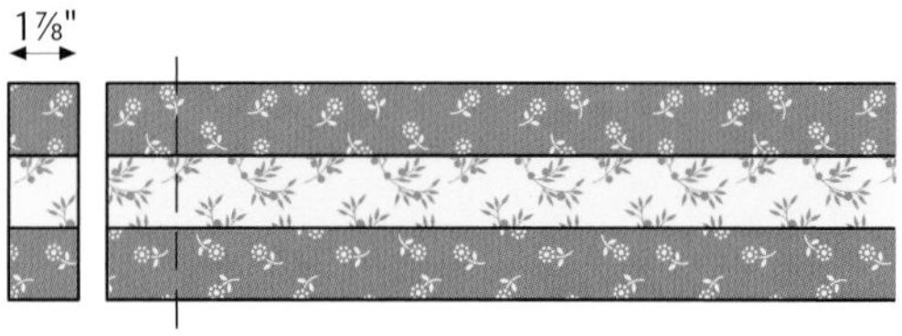

Strip set 2.
Make 1. Cut 10 segments.

2. Sew together two strip set 1 segments and one strip set 2 segment to make a Nine Patch A block. Press the seam allowances toward the top and bottom rows. Repeat to make a second Nine Patch A block.

    Sew together one strip set 1 segment and two strip set 2 segments to make a Nine Patch B block. Press the seam allowances toward the center row. Repeat to make a total of four Nine Patch B blocks. Both blocks should measure 4⅝" x 4⅝", including seam allowances.

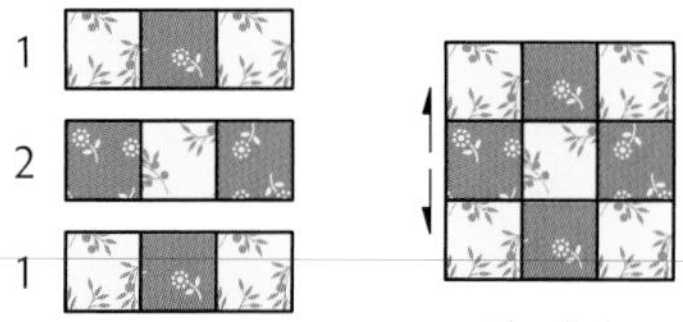

Block A.
Make 2.

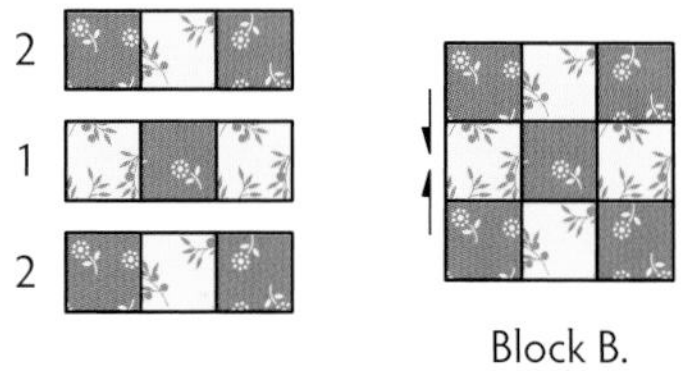

Block B.
Make 4.

ASSEMBLING THE QUILT TOP

1. Sew two A blocks, one B block, and two blue 1½" x 4⅝" sashing pieces in a column as shown in the assembly diagram below. Press the seam allowances toward the sashing. Repeat, using three B blocks to make a second column.

2. Join the columns, sewing one blue 1½" x 14⅞" sashing strip between the columns as shown to make the quilt center. Press the seam allowances toward the just-added sashing piece.

    Sew together three blue 1½" x 4⅝" pieces and two red 1½" squares to make a pieced sashing strip. Press the seam allowances toward the blue pieces. Repeat to make a second pieced sashing strip.

3. Add the pieced sashing strips to the long edges of the quilt center to make the quilt top. Press the seam allowances toward the pieced sashing strips.

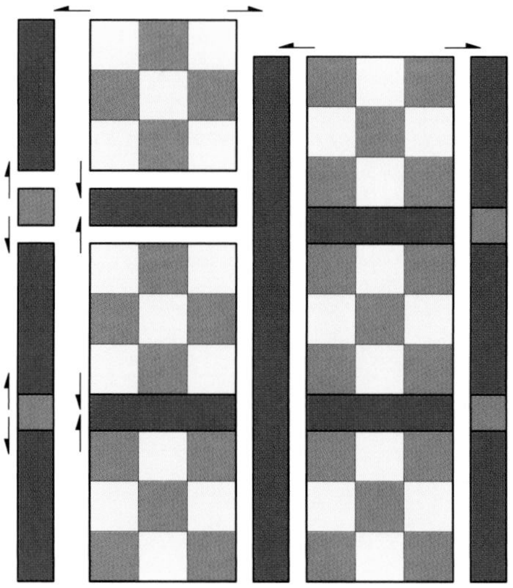

4. Trace the large-star pattern on page 51 twice and the small-star pattern once onto paper-backed fusible web. Follow the fusible-web manufacturer's directions for applying the fusible web to the gold wool 8" square. Referring to the photo on page 48 for placement, fuse the wool stars to the quilt top. (For more information on fusible appliqué, refer to "Fusible Appliqué" on page 60 or go to ShopMartingale.com/HowtoQuilt.) Hand or machine blanket-stitch the star appliqués in place to complete the quilt.

FINISHING THE QUILT

For more information on any of the following steps, refer to "Quiltmaking Basics" on page 56. You also can download free illustrated instructions about finishing your quilt at ShopMartingale.com/HowtoQuilt.

1. Layer and baste the quilt top, batting, and backing.

2. Quilt as desired. The sample is quilted on the sashing strips and squares, ¼" inside the seams.

3. Trim the backing and batting even with the quilt top. Add a hanging sleeve, if desired. (You will need a 2½" x 11" strip of coordinating fabric for a hanging sleeve. For more information about adding a hanging sleeve and a display hanger, see page 59.)

4. Using the red-and-white 2½"-wide strips, make and attach the binding to finish the edges of the quilt.

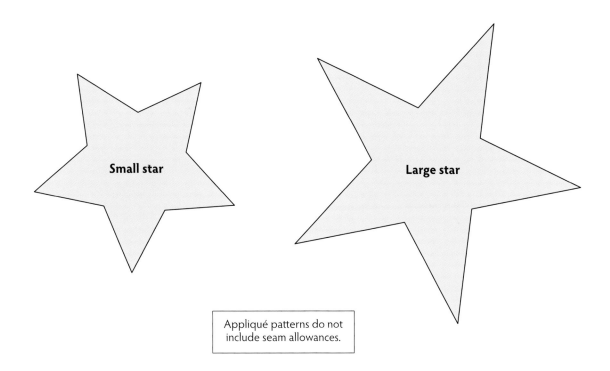

Small star

Large star

Appliqué patterns do not include seam allowances.

Patriotic Dreams

Throw pillows are favorite decorating accessories in any home. Stitch this Dresden Plate accent onto an easy-to-make envelope cover. It will look lovely displayed on your couch, chair, or bed. Make more than one!

"Patriotic Dreams," designed by Kathy Flowers

FINISHED PROJECT: 16" x 16"

★ ## MATERIALS

★ *Yardage is based on 42"-wide fabric.*

★ ½ yard of beige print for pillow cover

★ 21 rectangles, 2½" x 3½", of assorted red, white, and/or blue prints for large Dresden Plate blades

★ 21 rectangles, 2" x 2½", of assorted red, white, and/or blue prints for small Dresden Plate blades

★ 2 squares, 6" x 6", of red print for Dresden Plate center circle

★ 1 square, 4" x 4", of cream felted wool for star appliqué

★ Paper-backed fusible web

★ 16" pillow form*

★ 18"- or 24"-long ruler (or yardstick)

★ **Your pillow cover should measure a bit smaller than your pillow form for a good fit. If you want a very taut pillow, use ½" seam allowances rather than the standard ¼" seam allowances. Your completed pillow cover will then measure 15" x 15" for a standard 16" pillow form.*

★ ## CUTTING

From the red print, cut:
2 circles using the circle pattern

From *each* red, white, and/or blue print 2½" x 3½" rectangle, cut:
1 blade using the large-blade template pattern

From *each* red, white, and/or blue print 2" x 2½" rectangle, cut:
1 blade using the small-blade pattern

From the beige print, cut:
1 rectangle, 16" x 41"

★ ## ASSEMBLING THE DRESDEN PLATE APPLIQUÉ

1. With right sides together, sew the two red circles together, ¼" from the edges. Clip the seam allowances around the circle, being careful not to cut

into the seam. Carefully pull one layer away from the other and cut a large X through the center of the top layer. Turn the circle inside out through the X. Press.

2. Using the star pattern on page 55, trace one star shape onto the fusible web. Following the manufacturer's directions, adhere the fusible web to the cream wool 4" square. Cut out the star shape on the drawn lines. Fuse the wool star appliqué to the center of the red circle on the uncut side. Stitch a French knot at each inner and outer point of the star (10 French knots total) to appliqué it into place.

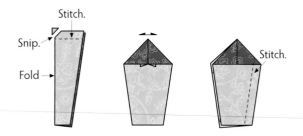

French knot

3. Fold each large-blade piece in half lengthwise and stitch a scant ¼" seam across the wide short ends. Backstitch to reinforce each tip; snip each angle as shown. Press the seam allowances open to reduce bulk. Turn each blade right side out. With right sides together, sew the blades together to form a circle. Repeat with the small blade pieces.

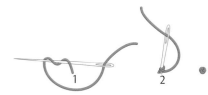

4. Layer the circle of small blades over the circle of large blades. Baste the circles together. Add the red center circle with the wool star appliqué atop and stitch in place to make a Dresden Plate appliqué.

ASSEMBLING THE ENVELOPE PILLOW COVER

1. On each short end of the beige 16" x 41" rectangle, fold over ¼" and press. Fold over again ¼" and stitch closed to make a hem.

2. With right sides together, insert a long ruler and fold one end of the fabric over the ruler to measure 12". (The 1" mark on the ruler will be inside the folded fabric.) Press the fold line in place or mark the fold line with pins.

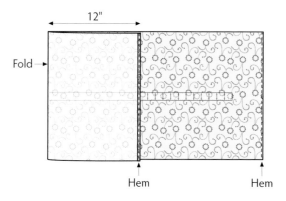

3. Remove the long ruler from inside the fabric and lay it along the outside of the folded piece of fabric. Fold the opposite side over until the pillow cover measures 15½". Press the fold line in place or mark the fold line with pins.

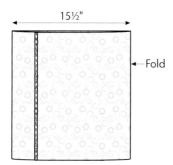

4. Lay the fabric open and center the Dresden Plate appliqué between the fold lines. Whipstitch in place.

5. Using the previously pressed (or pinned) fold lines, with right sides together, stitch along the long open sides, backstitching at each end and as you run across the inside hidden hems.

6. Turn the pillow cover inside out and insert the pillow form to complete the project.

★ ★ ★

Blade patterns do include seam allowances.

Large blade

Small blade

Star

Appliqué patterns do not include seam allowances.

Circle

★ ★ ★

Quiltmaking Basics

Did you come across an unfamiliar term or technique? In this section, you'll find a helpful glossary of terms plus illustrated instructions on various quiltmaking techniques.

QUILTMAKING GLOSSARY

Acrylic ruler. Use a clear acrylic ruler when cutting fabric. I recommend having at least two sizes: 6½" x 24" and 10½" square. I use Creative Grids rulers as they have embedded grip dots that help hold fabric in place while you cut, so there's no need to add more grips to the rulers.

Design wall. A design wall can be a valuable tool. It provides a place to hang your blocks as you piece them, so you can quickly see a mistake (if you make one) before sewing the blocks together. A design wall can save you precious time in the long run. You can purchase large design walls inexpensively (Fons & Porter makes a great one) or make a small one using leftover batting or flannel pinned to a piece of foam-core board.

Iron. Use a dry iron on cotton setting to press your seams. Do not use steam. Press on a flat surface such as an ironing board.

Pressing. This is the method used for setting a seam or pressing seam allowances in a certain direction. Press the hot iron down on a seam and then lift the iron up. The motion of the iron is up and down, not back and forth as you would do when ironing clothes to remove wrinkles.

Needles. Use needles as recommended by your machine manufacturer for machine piecing. You'll need basic hand-sewing needles for hand stitching the bindings to your quilts, and appliqué needles for attaching wool-appliqué pieces.

Pins. Use sharp pins to hold pieces in place.

Seam ripper. If and when you make a mistake (it's OK, we all do), a seam ripper is handy for removing the stitches. There are many on the market to choose from.

Rotary cutter. Safety first! The blade of the rotary cutter, which is razor sharp, should never be exposed until you are ready to cut fabric. A rotary cutter is used to accurately cut fabric to the desired size. A medium-sized cutter (45 mm) allows you to cut strips of fabric and trim small pieces.

Rotary-cutting (self-healing) mat. Purchase the largest mat you can afford that fits your work surface. If you must remove the mat from your work surface when not in use, store it flat to avoid warpage. Mats are expensive, and once warped, they normally can't be repaired; keep this in mind when storing.

Thread. The project you're working on will determine which thread to use. For piecing quilt blocks, 100% cotton thread is widely used. A thinner, high-quality thread such as Aurifil will result in a truer ¼" seam allowance. For wool appliqué, you can use DMC embroidery thread or one of many wool threads on the market, including Aurifil wool thread.

FINISHING THE QUILT

Refer to the following instructions for help with finishing your quilt.

Adding Borders

A border is often added to a quilt top to enhance the center design. If the center of the quilt is busy, such as in a scrappy quilt, a thin inner border gives the eye a place to rest before moving outward toward the final larger border of the quilt. A quilt border is often thought of as a frame to capture the beauty within, just as a picture frame captures the beauty of a portrait. It is the designer's choice how borders are used, and many factors are taken into consideration. Some quilts have no borders at all.

If borders are used, it's important to measure the quilt top prior to cutting the border strips. From the center of the quilt, measure in both directions, lengthwise and widthwise. Add the side border strips first and press the seam allowances toward the border strips. Add the top and bottom border strips last. Press the seam allowances toward the border strips.

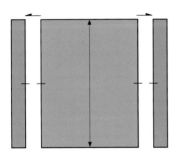

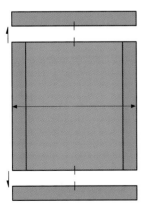

Preparing Quilt Layers

On a large flat surface, lay the quilt backing right side down. Use masking tape to hold it securely in place. Lay the batting of your choice over the quilt backing. Pay extra attention as you smooth out any wrinkles. Again, use masking tape to hold the batting in place. Lay the quilt top right side up and secure it with masking tape as well. Hand baste or pin the layers in place.

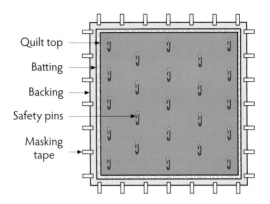

Quilting

Quilting the three layers of a quilt is what keeps the layers from shifting during use or when washing and drying. Small quilts are easily quilted either by hand or on a home sewing machine. An easy quilting method you can use when quilting by machine is "quilt in the ditch," where the machine needle falls into the seam allowance. Another method is "quilt outside the ditch," where the presser foot of the machine runs just along the seam allowance. Large quilts can be quilted on a home machine, if you're an experienced quilter, or sent out to a long-arm quilter who is a master at quilting on large machines made specifically for this purpose. Although their services are an added expense, long-arm quilters can turn your large, pretty quilt top into a masterpiece.

Binding

Follow these steps to successfully bind your quilts.

1. Join strips of fabric right sides together as shown on page 58, stitching at a 45° angle. Trim the seam allowances to ¼" and press open (not to one side). Pressing the seam allowances open creates a smooth,

continuous strip of fabric. With wrong sides together, fold the strip in half lengthwise and press.

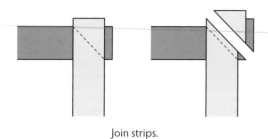

Join strips.

Press seam open.

2. Pin the binding strip in place along the edge of the quilt. Begin stitching approximately 15" from the end of the binding strip and stop ¼" from the corner of the quilt; backstitch.

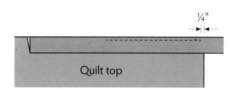

Quilt top

3. Remove the quilt from the machine and fold the binding up, so the crease forms a 45° angle, and then back down as shown. Place the quilt under the presser foot and begin stitching again. Backstitch. Continue sewing in this manner around the quilt.

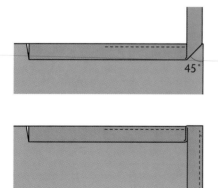

45°

4. Stop stitching and backstitch approximately 3" after completing the last corner on the side of the quilt where you began. Overlap the two ends, with the ending binding strip on the bottom. Trim the beginning binding strip so it lies 2¼" over the bottom binding strip.

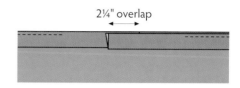

2¼" overlap

5. Lay the two strips at a 45° angle to each other and sew on the diagonal. Trim away the excess fabric and press the seam allowances open. Stitch the binding in place, backstitching at the beginning and end.

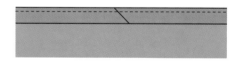

6. Turn the binding to the back and whipstitch it in place. Miter the corners of the binding as shown.

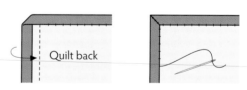

Quilt back

Hanging Sleeve

Cut a piece of fabric 4" wide and 2" shorter than the width of your quilt. Fold each short end over ¼" and stitch in place to hem. With right sides together, fold the fabric in half lengthwise and sew along the long raw edge. Press the seam allowances open to make a sleeve. Turn the sleeve inside out and press. Center the sleeve under the binding on the back of the quilt top; whipstitch in place along the top and bottom of the sleeve.

Quilt Hangers and Stands

Once I've added a hanging sleeve to my small quilts, I like to display them using Ackfeld hangers. Ackfeld Manufacturing handcrafts unique steel, powdered-coated, durable wire hangers for displaying quilts on the wall, floor, table, or door. For more information, visit their website at ackfeldwire.com.

I find that Ackfeld wire hangers are great for changing one's home decor from season to season or holiday to holiday. If you have a small birthday quilt, display it using an Ackfeld hanger and showcase it as a centerpiece for a child's birthday party. A small pink or blue quilt displayed in an Ackfeld hanger and posted to Facebook is also a great way to announce the birth of a new baby or grandchild!

See below and page 18 for examples of the small quilts that I've displayed on stands in my home.

LABELS

Although not necessary, labels are a wonderful way to identify many aspects of your quilt masterpiece. If the quilt is a gift, the label can identify who made the quilt, who it was made for, and the date. You can add as much or as little as you like to your label. Labels can be from plain muslin sewn into the binding. I use a micron-tipped archival marker to add information such as who pieced it, who quilted it, and the date. A large variety of quilt labels can be purchased online or at your local quilt shop.

> Your Name
> 2017

★ ★ ★

Fusible Appliqué

Fusible appliqué is just one method for attaching one decorative piece on top of another. In this book, the appliquéd pieces are made of felted wool. When using felted wool, your appliqué pieces have raw edges and there are no seam allowances as in needle-turned appliqué. Use your favorite stitch to accent the appliqué piece. There is no wrong stitch. It's the quilter's choice.

Using paper-backed fusible web is a fast and fun way to appliqué. One of the most important things to remember about fusible appliqué is that the appliqué patterns must be the reverse image of the image on the finished project. In this book, appliqué patterns that specify the fusible-appliqué method have already been reversed.

Refer to the manufacturer's directions when applying fusible web to your fabrics; each brand is a little different, and pressing too long may result in fusible web that doesn't stick well.

1. Trace or draw your shape onto the paper-backing side of the fusible web. Cut out the shape, leaving about a ¼" margin all around the outline.

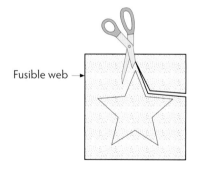

Fusible web →

2. Fuse the shape to the wrong side of your fabric.

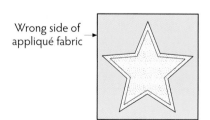

Wrong side of appliqué fabric

3. Cut out the shape exactly on the marked line.

4. Remove the paper backing; position the shape on the background and press it in place with your iron.

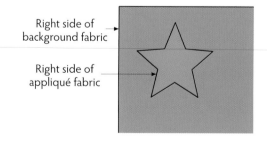

Right side of background fabric →

Right side of appliqué fabric →

5. If desired, add decorative stitches by hand, or machine stitch around the edges of the fused appliqués. Commonly used stitches include the satin stitch and blanket stitch.

★ ★ ★

Paper Foundation Piecing

Also known as paper piecing, paper foundation piecing is a technique in which fabric is sewn to a paper foundation. This method is often used to stitch difficult blocks that have many small pieces or challenging angles. Paper piecing results in accurate star points and ¼" seam allowances because the stitch line is printed on the paper.

Basically, paper foundation piecing involves printing or tracing your block pattern onto a piece of easy-to-tear paper. Then you *sew fabric pieces to the wrong side of the paper,* using the lines on the right side of the paper for guidance. Because you're sewing on the line and using a firm foundation for stability, the sewing is precise and accurate. When all the sewing is complete, you tear away the paper, and your beautiful block remains.

Paper-piecing paper is available at your local quilt store and online. The best paper tears easily along the stitching lines, doesn't leave a bunch of little fibers behind, and is strong enough that it won't fall apart and jam the photocopier. The foundation paper also needs to be translucent enough that you can see fabric pieces through the paper when you hold it up to the light.

In these foundation patterns from "Americana Coasters" and "Eldorado," the solid lines are the sewing lines, and the solid line around the perimeter indicates the edge of the finished block. The dashed outer line of the pattern indicates the outer ¼" seam allowance used to sew this block to others in the quilt, as in "Eldorado," or to a backing square, as in "Americana Coasters."

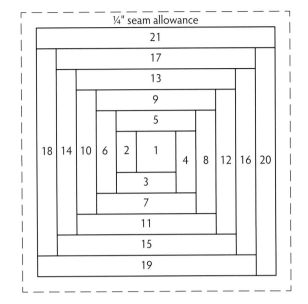

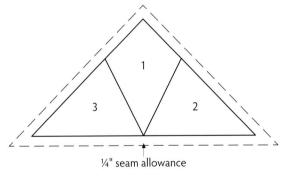

If you've used a lightweight foundation paper—such as Martingale's *Papers for Foundation Piecing,* tissue paper, or baking parchment—and you've set your stitch length to be short, try this technique for releasing the paper: Hold the block firmly with one hand on each side of a stitching line. Give the block a quick tug in opposite directions. The fabric is flexible and will give, while the paper is firm and will snap. This works well on longer seams, but you may still need to use tweezers in areas where multiple seams come together, such as in narrow points.

About the Author

Kathy Flowers began quilting in 1976, making doll quilts for her daughter. She started designing quilts in 2008 and sold her patterns exclusively to a local quilt shop before offering them for publication in 2012 to *McCall's Quilting* magazine.

Kathy believes that inspiration is not only visual but comes from within: it's a feeling. Kathy has been crafting and designing something for as long as she can remember. Whether it's a flower garden or a quilt, she sees design all around her, sometimes in the movement of nature, like butterflies, or in still structures. She can also look at a fabric and remember a kindness shown to her from someone in her past, and design from that.

Kathy's designs continue to be published in *McCall's Quilting* as well as in other internationally distributed magazines. Her quilt kits and patterns are available on her website, PiecesofDreams-Kathy.com. You may also visit Kathy on Facebook at Pieces of Dreams Quilt Designs and on Twitter @PODquilts.

Acknowledgments

I have been blessed with many talented and kind individuals in my life. I am forever grateful for the footprints of their love, their kindness, and the generosities they have willingly and selflessly shared with me.

A special thanks to my sister, Patty Winkler, for the use of her design "Leo's Star." It is Patty who officially toots my horn. She first introduced me to the art of quilting in 1976 and has been my inspiration over the years. Patty encourages me to think outside the box. She taught me to see the block before seeing the whole quilt, and when I said, "I can't do that," it was Patty who always said, "Yes you can!" Everybody should have a sister like her.

Thank you to Jo Beth Simons for the use of her design "Stars of Freedom." Jo Beth hails from across the street during my childhood. Reconnecting on Facebook, we share our love of quilting and numerous childhood memories like catching lightning bugs, jumping rope, and having Kool-Aid stands.

Vonnie Johnson, every time I hand you a quilt top, to you it's like a fresh new canvas—and without fail, you hand me back a masterpiece! You never cease to amaze me. Thank you for your never-ending talent and your friendship.

A heartfelt thank-you goes to Beth Hayes, Editor-in-Chief Emeritus, and Susan Guzman, Content Director, at *McCall's Quilting*. Your kind words, in acceptance and rejection, have guided me to where I am today. From the bottom of my heart, I thank you both.

And last, but certainly not least, thank you to all the military men and women, regardless of your post, at home and abroad, who tirelessly serve and sacrifice for our great nation to keep us free. Whether you sit at a desk or serve in the front lines of war, it is because of you, the men and women before you, and those who will come after you, that we are allowed such simple and often taken-for-granted freedoms to pursue our hobbies. This simple thank-you hardly seems adequate.